Sacred Hearts

by Sue Glover

fairplay press

First published by fairplay press, an imprint of Capercaillie Books Limited in 2009.

Registered office 1 Rutland Court, Edinburgh.

Printed in the UK.

A catalogue record for this book is available from the British Library.

ISBN 978-1-906220-33-4

The publisher acknowledges support from the Scottish Arts Council towards the publication of this title.

Scottish
Arts Council

Sacred Hearts

Sue Glover was born in Edinburgh and lives in the East Neuk of Fife. She writes for radio, television and theatre. As well as *Sacred Hearts*, her theatre work includes *The Bubble Boy*, *The Straw Chair*, *Bondagers*, *The Seal Wife*, *Artist Unknown*, and *Shetland Saga*. The Traverse Theatre revived its production of *Bondagers* three times, and took it to London, and Canada. Several of her plays have been translated and produced in Europe and the United States. Her television work includes *Homefront*, *The Bubble Boy*, *The Spaver Connection*, *Dear Life*, *Mrs Miller and Madame Montand*, and work for *Take the High Road* and *Strathblair*. Radio work includes adaptations as well as original work, the most recent an adaptation of Tove Jansson's *Fair Play*.

fairplay press

Introduction

In 1975 the prostitutes of Lyons were protesting against lack of protection from a 'Lyons Ripper'. That same year the 'Yorkshire Ripper' murdered his first victim in Chapeltown, Leeds. Five years and thirteen murders later, the Yorkshire murderer was arrested. The Lyons killer was never discovered, although the murders ceased after the protest. The play was inspired by the events of Lyons, Bradford, and Leeds; and based – loosely – on the Lyons strike. It is about a group of women seeking sanctuary in a climate of violence and fear, such as everyone in Britain was aware of in the years leading up to Sutcliffe's arrest. All the characters, onstage and off, are fictitious.

'I walk the babysitter to her place and then run all the way home, down the middle of the road, with my little knife in my hand, in my running shoes.' (Single parent quoted in *The Guardian* during the Yorkshire Ripper investigation.)

'He has made it clear that he hates prostitutes. Many people do. We, as a police force, will continue to arrest prostitutes. But the Ripper is now killing innocent girls.' (Senior Police Officer at press conference during Yorkshire Ripper investigation.)

A prostitute, during the Yorkshire Ripper Investigation, was violently attacked. Other prostitutes came to her aid. 'Sitting watching were policemen in a car who made no effort to intervene. When one of the women ran screaming to the police car for help, they told her they had been instructed not to move, that they were there to collect car numbers. The attacker got away.' (David Yallop, *Deliver Us From Evil*.)

'If a young lady chooses to get into bed with a married man she can't expect to be treated with the reverence of a mother superior of a convent.' (George Carmen, Q.C.)

'In non-monetary societies such as those of Africa, prostitution appears unknown before European contact and or urbanization, and erotic depictions do not have the pornographic functions they have in monetary economies.' (Ned Polsky, *On the Sociology of Pornography*.)

Sue Glover 2009

Characters

(Brief biographical details of the women are revealed in the final scene, when we hear the court sentences.)

JOJO:	in her fifties or sixties.
DANIELLE	in her thirties, with two small children. Practical, blunt. Doesn't dress provocatively.
LEILA:	in her thirties, quite glamorous.
THERESE:	Seventeen. Been fighting authority since primary school, and meets violence with violence.
BRIGITTE:	fourteen or fifteen, a runaway from a 'good' background.
FATHER GAILLAC:	young parish priest.
RAYMOND:	sacristan. Mid-thirties or older. A loner, a mis-fit.
POLICE INSPECTOR: MAN AT CONFESSION: INTRUDER IN CHURCH:	these can be played by the actor who plays Raymond
TWO YOUNG MOTHERS: YOUNG HOUSEWIFE: EXCITED MAN: FAMILY VALUES MAN: VICIOUS WOMAN: EXCITED MAN:	these can be played by members of the cast

Setting

The set should be minimal, as the scenes sometimes merge one into the other. A too defined set would inhibit the action. The audience has to have the impression that this is one of several small chapels of a large church, and that somewhere beyond the stage is the nave.

Most scenes take place in this chapel. Others take place elsewhere in the church; in the street outside the church; and by the confessional. I had thought of the confessional as being of a semi-closed design, that is the priest sits facing the audience, with a grill, curtain or partition obscuring his view to left and right. It is behind these partitions that the penitents would come to confess. But in the original production chairs were moved about the stage to convey different things at different times, and were used to create the impression of a confessional as required.

Act 1

Scene 1

Early morning. The chapel is very dimly lit. The heavy double doors of the church are heard offstage as they slam shut.

DANIELLE, LEILA, THERESE and JOJO enter. We hear their voices without being able to identify the speakers.

JOJO: Oh, God, what's that?

DANIELLE: The doors.

LEILA: Five o'clock. Denise said we'd lock ourselves in at 5 o'clock.

VOICES: **(offstage, shouting down the nave)** No-one leaves! No-one leaves!

Some lights come on in the church. The girls look at each other, triumphant.

THE WOMEN: **(a pact)** No-one leaves!

THERESE: Anyone got a drink?

DANIELLE: This time of the morning? Nothing doing!

JOJO: Morning! It's still the middle of the night. **(Shouting up the nave.)** Nicole? Martine? Anyone over there got a drink?

BRIGITTE comes on, unnoticed, stands watching them.

DANIELLE: Hope you brought supplies of your own, girl.

THERESE: Didn't have time, did I?

LEILA: You should have made time, the rest of us did.

JOJO: **(pulls a bottle from one of her bags)** Hey! Therese!

THERESE goes over to her. Takes a swig from the bottle, or JOJO pulls out a glass or beaker from her bags.

THERESE: **(not to JOJO)** What about a joint then? Leila – you must have –

DANIELLE: **(stern)** No drugs!

JOJO: Rules are rules.

THERESE: Fuck the rules.

BRIGITTE is still apart from them, watching, unnoticed.

JOJO: Therese!

DANIELLE: Therese! Therese! What else is there to do in here? **(Eye's LEILA's cigarette. If anyone's got a joint it'll be LEILA.)** Anyone got a fag, then? Um? Anyone?

LEILA: Didn't you even bring a packet of fags, then? **(But hands her the one she's already lit, and lights herself another.)**

THERESE: I brought a torch, and some batteries, which is more than you did. And I brought my knife.

DANIELLE: You would! What about a toothbrush?

THERESE: Sure, I've got a toothbrush. **(She notices BRIGITTE.)** Hop it, fishface – go on!

JOJO: Therese!

THERESE: There's plenty room down the other end of the church – there's other chapels – this one's booked.

DANIELLE gives her a nudge, Therese without even glancing at her, retaliates – but continues to stare out BRIGITTE.

THERESE: We bagged Our Lady's Chapel – right? The girls from Zola Street.

JOJO: **(coming in over this)** There's plenty room –

THERESE: So bugger off, okay?

DANIELLE: Hey – let's have some solidarity here!

THERESE: What?

LEILA: We're on strike, we're all on strike.

DANIELLE: There's room for one more, for heaven's sake.

THERESE: We bagged Our Lady.

DANIELLE: **(to BRIGITTE)** Take a pew – if you want.

They are busy unpacking, setting up camp. JOJO's baggage includes a six-pack of cheap wine. BRIGITTE doesn't move.

THERESE: **(to BRIGITTE)** Still here?

BRIGITTE doesn't answer.

LEILA: Where do you work, then?

BRIGITTE: Zola Street.

THERESE: Since when?

JOJO: Let her alone. There's plenty room here – and room to spare on Zola Street, too, for all that –

THERESE: **(in over this)** Is there fuck!

JOJO aims a swipe in her direction. THERESE threatens an

answering blow – but JOJO is the one person she'd never land one on.

JOJO: **(to THERESE)** Don't mind her, doll.

DANIELLE: What do they call you?

BRIGITTE: Brigitte.

THERESE: **(in over this)** Where on Zola Street? Where do you work on Zola Street?

LEILA: Oh, Cara mentioned you! She said there was a new girl at the Cockatoo. You work the lane behind the Cafe Cockatoo.

JOJO: Take a chair, doll – take a couple, whatever you need. Our Lady belongs to everyone.

BRIGITTE: I only came for the meeting.

LEILA: It's a sit-in, not a meeting.

THERESE: Where's your gear? Is that all you've got?

LEILA: You should have brought a sleeping bag.

DANIELLE: It's going to be a long meeting.

JOJO: Have you not even brought a blanket? It's chilly in here. Couldn't she just nip out smartish, and fetch –

DANIELLE: No.

JOJO: It's not even light yet outside –

DANIELLE and LEILA: No-one leaves.

BRIGITTE: But – I have to go to work later on. This evening. I need the money.

LEILA: We all have to work, pet.

THERESE: We can't work in here.

She and JOJO laugh.

LEILA: We can't work out there either – streets crawling with cops.

DANIELLE: A nutter on the loose.

LEILA: They booked me three times last night.

JOJO: Why don't they book the Ripper, eh?

LEILA: Why don't they search for Genevieve?

THERESE: **(to BRIGITTE)** Heard about Genevieve, have you?

BRIGITTE: The one that's missing? Yes.

THERESE: **(to BRIGITTE)** Got a drink on you, have you?

DANIELLE: It's breakfast time. **(to BRIGITTE)** Don't listen to her.

THERESE: Anything to eat?

BRIGITTE: I've got some spice-cake. It's quite fresh, I only bought it yesterday. **(Looking in her bag.)**

DANIELLE: Don't let eat her way through your larder. We'll be organising breakfast for everyone in a minute.

BRIGITTE offers some cake (it comes in sticky packets, ready sliced) to THERESE.

THERESE: This is the best spot in the church. You're in luck. Radiator, carpets. Toilets just over there.

LEILA: We'll find you a blanket or a coat or something. The committee'll have some extra. (. . .) Did Cara tell you about Genevieve? She used to work that lane – behind the Cockatoo.

JOJO: You're quite safe in here, pet.

JOJO: Safe as houses in here. Well, if you're not safe in Our Lady's Chapel, then you're not –

Heavy thuds from outside, on the church doors.

VOICE(S): **(offstage, from further down the church)** It's the cops. It's the cops.

LOUDHAILER: **(offstage, outside the church, the words need not be clear)** All unauthorised personnel out of the church. All unauthorised personnel out of the church.

THERESE: Fuck off!

LOUDHAILER: **(outside)** Everybody on the street. Everybody on the street.

JOJO: **(shouting)** Sorry, Monsieur – we've all got a headache!

A single dull thud. The group draws together. Another great thud.

VOICES: **(offstage, further down the church)** Doors! Doors!

VOICE: **(offstage)** Everybody on the doors!

They rush off, save for JOJO and BRIGITTE. BRIGITTE hesitates, looks to JOJO for guidance. But JOJO has crossed herself, and started to pray (hurriedly) to Our Lady. Thuds continue – or maybe a police siren. Hastily rounding off her prayer, JOJO signals to BRIGITTE, or takes her hand or arm, and hurries her off.

Scene 2

RAYMOND has taken a break from his floor-sweeping (he has one of those outsize brush-mops used in hospitals, railway stations,etc.) in order to complain to FATHER GAILLAC.

RAYMOND: Sleeping bags. Primus stoves. Radios. Clothes hanging all over the place. Lingerie, Father! There's a hammock in the organ loft.

FATHER GAILLAC: They have to sleep somewhere.

RAYMOND: A pisspot up there, too. No – I'm telling you, Father – on top of Verdi's Requiem.

FATHER GAILLAC: There are forty or so women in the church, Raymond. And only three toilets.

RAYMOND: And what am I doing? Cleaning after them. Cleaning up – female trash!

FATHER GAILLAC: They've scrubbed our little kitchenette from top to bottom, Raymond. It looks like new.

RAYMOND: The kitchen – oh, well, yes. What about the rest of the church? What about the altar? They've no business near –

FATHER GAILLAC: They haven't set foot in the altar area, Raymond, they treat the altar with the greatest respect.

RAYMOND: And what about the toilets?

FATHER GAILLAC: I've had a complaint about your presence in the – cloakrooms, Raymond.

RAYMOND: I have my job to do –

FATHER GAILLAC: The women would rather make it their job while they're here.

RAYMOND: So I should hope, I've got enough on my – **(It dawns.)** – 'while they're here'? How long are they going to be here then?

FATHER GAILLAC: **(not too happy about it himself)** God's house belongs to everyone.

RAYMOND: A strike! That's political, Father, nothing to do with religion. What are they striking for? More pay? Ha, ha. I'll give them more pay.

FATHER GAILLAC: They're frightened. They're in danger.

RAYMOND: From arrest, most of them. That's why the cops are three deep outside.

FATHER GAILLAC: Eight women murdered, and another one missing, almost certainly dead.

RAYMOND: Well, they know what to do then, don't they? Keep off the streets! Half naked! What do they expect? **(FATHER GAILLAC at a loss as to how to check this criticism.)** Why'd they choose our church? It isn't the biggest.

FATHER GAILLAC: We said mass here for the women who were murdered. We said prayers here for the girl who's missing.

RAYMOND: Ripper eight, police nil. And still they won't learn! **(Not directly to FATHER GAILLAC, but so that he can hear.)** You're soft on them, Father. **(HE starts sweeping, moving just too far off for the FATHER to distinguish the words.)** They're scum . . . scum. . .

He sweeps with his broom, sweeps into the next scene.

Scene 3

Out on the street.

Time: days earlier, shortly before the strike/sit in.

RAYMOND sweeping the street outside the church. The GIRLS are out on the street. RAYMOND stops to unwrap some chewing-gum. He looks the girls up and down, half scornful, half intimidated.

RAYMOND: Zola Street! They're in every doorway. Round the clock! What am I supposed to do? Walk the long way round to work? Ten minutes extra the long way round? Twenty minutes a day? Just to avoid Zola Street? **(He walks amongst them. BRIGITTE stands slightly apart from the others, not noticed by them, studying them.)** Well, I won't. No. I'll run the scum on Zola Street.

The GIRLS are putting on/adjusting their 'armour' – the masks and disguises that are their only protection while working. They check stockings, adjust a cleavage, a beret, repair make-up. But they are, at the same time, adjusting psychologically, taking on the 'role'.

JOJO: Hello, love.

BRIGITTE: **(trying the phrase out to herself)** Hello, love, I'm Brigitte.

JOJO: It's eighty for sex.

RAYMOND: I walk right past.

But he is staring at them, walking around them, not past them.

JOJO: A hundred for french and sex.

LEILA: A hundred for french and sex.

JOJO: A bit more for uniform and fancy business.

LEILA: Specialist services to be negotiated.

RAYMOND's lines cut across the GIRLS' lines.

RAYMOND: I stare them down.

BRIGITTE: **(bolder)** Hello, I'm Brigitte. Eighty in the car, right? A hundred back at my place.

LEILA: **(as RAYMOND comes near she puts a hand on his arm, or his shoulder, softly)** Excuse me, money first, my friend. **(She puts her hand in his pocket, and takes a note.)** That's the rule, money first. **(Tucks the note into her bra.)** Money first.

BRIGITTE: **(a foreign accent)** Hello there, I'm Brigitta. Would you like to ride with Brigitta?

RAYMOND takes note of Brigitte, looks her up and down. But now the others are retreating – back into the 'Church area', with one or two mutters of 'money first'. Except for BRIGITTE, who goes offstage.

RAYMOND: A disgrace to their sex. An insult to my mother. Don't tell me they can't get work. My mother worked. She worked in the mill. There were five of us at home. We never tasted meat. She cooked, cleaned, sewed. She never had a new coat. The priest called her a saint. An example, he said, a good woman, above rubies. (. . .) The old man ruled her with a rod of iron. Ruled us all, even the girls. Especially the girls. The big stick. The rod of iron.

Scene 4

JOJO is having a quiet tipple. THERESE is with her.

JOJO: That young Brigitte, she's pregnant.

THERESE: How would you know?

JOJO: She's been coughing her guts out in the toilets.

THERESE: That'll be why she's run away.

JOJO: Go easy on her – I mean it. She's only a kid, and she's one of us now if she's working Zola Street –

The others come in over the last half of this: BRIGITTE ahead, LEILA and DANIELLE carrying the banner.

BRIGITTE: **(enjoying herself)** Look at this! Look at this!

JOJO: What's going on?

LEILA: Banners for the Church.

BRIGITTE: We're hanging banners all over the church.

DANIELLE: This one's for our chapel.

The banner reads: 'No Fines, No Brothels, No Pimps'. They start to hang it up.

JOJO: What did Father Gaillac say?

BRIGITTE: He said it was okay.

JOJO: I thought the banner was to be outside the church?

LEILA: The girls from Market Street are doing one for outside.

BRIGITTE: These are for when anyone comes into the church. Press, and politicians.

LEILA: The Minister for Women's Affairs!

DANIELLE: The Minister of the Interior!

BRIGITTE: And we've all to have a good think about the charter.

DANIELLE: We've got to make a list of points for the committee meeting.

JOJO: Tonight?

LEILA: The Press Conference is tomorrow. Seven o'clock.

JOJO: In the morning?

DANIELLE: We have to get it out for morning radio, and telly – and the evening papers. We want to get the message out fast.

LEILA: Hell, yes, we don't want to stay cooped up in here forever.

JOJO: **(quietly)** I don't know, I wouldn't mind.

LEILA and DANIELLE are still fixing the banner.

LEILA: Brigitte, where's the clipboard? Brigitte's going to write our contributions down. **(Pause.)** Come on – what are we on strike for?

JOJO: We want the cops to find the ripper. **(To BRIGITTE.)** Go on, you write that down.

BRIGITTE: **(writing)** And jobs! We need jobs!

THERESE: We've got jobs! Cretin! Hadn't you noticed?

DANIELLE: Somewhere safe to work.

LEILA: **(drily)** A first-class hotel! Somewhere like the Hotel Leopold!

DANIELLE: We want the cops to stop raiding the bars and hotels.

BRIGITTE: **(writing)** No more hassle from the cops.

JOJO: You can't write that – not on a charter –

THERESE: It's true –

DANIELLE AND LEILA: **(more or less together)** Write it down.

BRIGITTE: I'm putting your names down beside each point – all right? ' – ' What's your other name, ?

DANIELLE: The things we want are: equality – for ourselves and our families; justice; and some decent health-care, that wouldn't come amiss. What we don't want are: prison sentences, police harassement, state-run brothels. . . .And pimps. . .

THERESE: I want a house, and a garden, and lots of money, and a swimming pool – **(To BRIGITTE, jokingly.)** Got a swimming pool, have you?

BRIGITTE shakes her head.

THERESE: **(a sudden intuition)** You bloody have, haven't you? She has! I bet she has!

BRIGITTE is shaking her head.

THERESE: What else you got? Got a nice hi-fi? Got a pony, have you? Got a bun in the –

JOJO: Zip it, you!

THERESE: **(pulling the clipboard from BRIGITTE)** Anyway, the charter's probably already written. Nicole asked us fifty questions when we arrived this morning, and Juliette wrote it all down.

LEILA: **(pulling the clipboard from THERESE)** It's not Juliette's charter, it's ours – everybody's.

JOJO: **(tired, and slightly inebriated)** Imagine me being on strike! Me! I never close!

LEILA: **(writes)** No taxes.

DANIELLE: I got a tax reminder yesterday. According to the government I have been a 'kept woman' for the last five years!

LEILA: Kept. Wish I was!

DANIELLE: Well, you were, weren't you?

LEILA: Kept? Shackled more like!

DANIELLE: **(writing)** No pimps.

THERESE: **(to BRIGITTE)** Indoors or out? (. . .) The swimming pool? Is it indoors or out?

BRIGITTE: There isn't any pool.

THERESE: Whose baby is it?

BRIGITTE: Mine.

THERESE: Virgin birth?

BRIGITTE: Boy-friend.

THERESE: Boy-friend with a swimming-pool?

BRIGITTE: Shut up about the pool, okay? (. . .) His daddy's got a pool, his daddy's got everything. When you've got just about everything already, you think you can buy the rest. Anything – anybody.

THERESE: Like you, you mean?

BRIGITTE: Not me. My baby. They're not getting their hands on my baby.

LEILA and DANIELLE busy with the clipboard. Giggling.

DANIELLE: Sisterhood!

LEILA: Oh, sure! Sisterhood.

DANIELLE: Solidarity.

THERESE starts to sing/hum a few bars of the Marseillaise.

LEILA: **(Joining in.)** We're here because we're here because – because the cops are over there. They're over there, they're over there, they're over theeere –

LEILA and DANIELLE join in. And, eventually, BRIGITTE also.

Because we're here because we're here because we're heee-er,
Because the cops are over there, they're over there –

They notice JOJO has fallen asleep, THERESE still holding her bottle or glass. They take it from her hand. takes a swig, offers it to BRIGITTE, then grabs it back before BRIGITTE can taste it.

THERESE: No, you're pregnant.

Someone still humming the song. They are settling for the night. A silence.

LEILA: **(hearing some sound)** What's that?

THERESE: The Ripper!

DANIELLE: Oh, shut up! Get some sleep.

Scene 5

Out on the street.

INSPECTOR: Not a whore on the street. No sign of the body, either. Genevieve David. That's the cow that bit me once when I shoved her in the cells. Good-looking cow. Great tits. I like a bit of a struggle – especially at the end of a shift. It's a turn on, maybe all you'll get if the wife's asleep when you get home. You'd have to like it rough to get it from Genevieve. No sense of humour. Crossed her legs. Packed a punch. I slapped her about a bit. That kind needs a slap. I bet she gave the Ripper a run for his money. (. . .) Great tits, though. (. . .) Not a slag on the street. How the hell do we find the Ripper without any bait?

Scene 6

Church bell is tolling, a single note. JOJO and DANIELLE come in pushing a laden trolley – food, coffee, even bouquets of flowers. The others are waking up, or coming back from the washroom.

DANIELLE: Breakfast! Come on, Zola Street, stuff yourselves! Coffee, apricots, chocolate, bread, cheese, croissants.

LEILA: Where's all this from?

DANIELLE: Jo Public.

LEILA: Here's to Jo!

THERESE: Rum babas!

BRIGITTE: Someone's sent flowers!

JOJO: **(taking the flowers)** These are for Our Lady.

THERESE: Okay, okay, okay.

JOJO: **(taking flowers over to the Madonna)** The rum babas are for Nicole. And Juliette. They were on watch by the doors all night.

They are helping themselves. FATHER GAILLAC comes in with an extra coffee pot. They don't notice him.

DANIELLE: The croissants are from the baker on the corner.

LEILA: He needn't think he's getting cheap rates next week.

THERESE: Filthy beast!

JOJO: No, it was his wife brought the croissants, I saw her at the door.

THERESE: Very fitting.

LEILA: Yes, she owes us a few favours!

JOJO: The things that man wants done with cream cakes!

FATHER GAILLAC advances with the coffee.

THERESE: Oh, good morning, Father.

FATHER GAILLAC: Bon appetit!

HE goes. LEILA is unwrapping a large chocolate-box type parcel.

BRIGITTE: Chocolates!

THERESE: Dog shit?

LEILA: **(opening the box)** Johnnies.

THERESE: From the baker?

BRIGITTE: The baker's wife?

DANIELLE: The fuzz?

LEILA: The press?

DANIELLE: The Inland Revenue?

LEILA: **(holding a packet up to the light)** Daren't use them, that's for sure. Someone'll have stuck a pin through every packet, I'll bet.

THERESE: It's a plant! 'In church, with a hundred packets of condoms? – You're booked!'

BRIGITTE: Well, they're not going to arrest anyone for carrying condoms!

DANIELLE: It's a criminal offence, Brigitte.

BRIGITTE: **(shrugs)** I've never bought them anyhow.

She dips her croissant in coffee. A silence. She eats hungrily . . . only gradually aware of the disapproval.

LEILA: Listen. From now on, you buy them.

DANIELLE: First rule: get the money. Second rule: break open a rubber.

LEILA: Keep them in your bag – or better still, your shoes, or your bra.

DANIELLE: Some of those punters are scum – you don't know what you might catch – and they're glad to pass it on.

THERESE: You'll get offered more for doing it without –

DANIELLE: But you don't!

JOJO: Ah, poor kid – you've put her off her croissant. She wasn't to know.

LEILA: She knows now.

JOJO: She's just a kid.

LEILA: Not any more.

JOJO: **(pushes the trolley off – we hear her call as she disappears)** 'Anyone for more grub? Still some here, girls! Croissants – cigarettes – apricots – chocolate! Got to keep your strength up!'

DANIELLE: You know that cop with the funny eye? The one that books you without even leaving his car? He wound down his window the other night, held out his hand for my bag, picked out the johnnies. My night's supply. 'See these?' he says to his driver, and the two of them go: 'Ha, ha, ha, ha.' Hilarious. And his driver takes his fag out his mouth and goes: pop, pop, pop! Every packet burned through. 'Good night, darling', he says. 'I won't book you this time – this is just a caution.'

LEILA: I hate when they call you 'darling'.

DANIELLE: I hate them full stop. **(To Brigitte.)** Watch out for him.

BRIGITTE: With a funny eye?

DANIELLE: Yes. Anyone new to the district – he'll have sex with them first – then flash his I.D.

BRIGITTE: He already did.

A silence.

LEILA: In his car?

Brigitte nods.

THERESE: How much?

BRIGITTE: Fifteen.

LEILA: For how long?

BRIGITTE: **(after a pause)** A while.

THERESE: What? How long?

BRIGITTE: A while. Quite a while.

They hiss in sympathy.

THERESE: **(cracking her knuckles loudly)** Call yourself a pro!

BRIGITTE: He said I'm on the register now: common prostitute. I have to be in court tomorrow morning.

Laughter.

LEILA: Honey, we're all due in court tomorrow – or the next day.

DANIELLE: Due in prison, most of us.

LEILA: That's why we're here – on strike.

BRIGITTE: I thought you were here because of the Ripper?

DANIELLE: We're here because the cops aren't looking for the Ripper.

LEILA: They keep booking us instead.

DANIELLE: Why hunt the Ripper, he's got hammers and knives, and screwdrivers? He's dangerous! Round up the tarts instead!

LEILA: We don't fight back.

THERESE: Not much!

DANIELLE: Unless we're pissed –

THERESE: Or stoned, maybe.

JOJO comes back, without the trolley, carrying a mug and a croissant for herself.

LEILA: Twenty, thirty arrests a night. It looks brilliant on paper, it leads to promotion, it makes them feel good. It makes them feel strong. And we're led away like lambs – oh, maybe we scratch and swear and scream a bit –

THERESE: **(muttering)** A bit? Speak for yourself!

DANIELLE: – but we don't hit folk over the head with a hammer, slit their stomachs, tie their legs behind their necks and wait till their knee joints burst –

JOJO: **(in over this)** Stop that, stop it! There's no need for that, Danielle. You ought to be ashamed.

LEILA: Ashamed? We ought to be ashamed?

DANIELLE: Genevieve was a friend of mine.

JOJO: **(in over this, not heeding it)** In front of the kid!

LEILA: Of course in front of the kid. She's got to know, she's got to –

JOJO: **(in over this)** We're safe in here. It's lovely: friends and food, and not rushing out to turn another trick. Time for a natter, and the Father left the heating on last night, and the water's hot. We need to rest up.

DANIELLE: Genevieve, Natalie, Sonia, Mimi, they were my friends, I stood beside them on the street. Elli, Lola, Raquel, Eva, Liliane – beautiful Liliane: I've cadged fags off them, sat in the cop shop with them, slept in the cells with them. . .

JOJO: **(in over this)** We need a bit of a holiday.

LEILA: **(more gently than DANIELLE)** This is a protest, Jojo, a campaign. You've seen the papers! We're news! They care about Genevieve now –

DANIELLE: A bit late!

LEILA: They never gave a toss about Liliane and the others. Maybe now they'll start to think a bit about us. We're only trying to make a living.

JOJO: Just don't keep making out all johns are bastards and rippers, okay? Because they're not.

DANIELLE snorts with derision.

I've got some very nice clients.

DANIELLE: Lucky old you.

JOJO: That guy Marco – a proper gentleman – he paid my hospital bills, he sent me flowers.

DANIELLE: More than your Maurice did.

JOJO: **(quick as a flash)** Maurice sent me roses.

DANIELLE: **(low)** It was us sent you the roses, doll.

JOJO: Maurice came every day . . . well, most days. He came when he could.

DANIELLE: Buggered off for good when you turned real poorly, though, didn't he? When he saw you wouldn't be on the game again for a while.

JOJO: Well, he's back now.

DANIELLE and THERESE mutter, exchange looks.

JOJO: I've got some really lovely regulars.

No-one is convinced.

If you treat them polite, they do likewise.

LEILA: The overalls might – not the city suits, though.

JOJO: Marco wears a suit.

LEILA: Ah, well – if only they were all like Marco!

DANIELLE: Yeah, Marco's lovely. Bloody lovely!

LEILA: I'd give it away to Marco!

DANIELLE: He wouldn't thank you for it! He can only get his rocks off he he has to pay!

JOJO: There's no need to be nasty about a gentleman like Marco. It's not his fault.

DANIELLE: Whose is it, then? His mother's, I suppose? Or his wife's? Whose side are you on, anyway?

JOJO: Side? What side? What do you mean: 'side'?

DANIELLE: Every time you take a shine to your clients – usually the posh ones – you start slagging off their women folk.

JOJO: Would I? Would I? Who says I would?

DANIELLE: Ever heard of women's lib, Jojo?

JOJO: I'm not burning my bra!

LEILA: That'd be some fire!

DANIELLE: If they ever catch the Ripper you'll probably say it was his mother's fault! Or his wife's. That's what's wrong with cops too, I suppose?

JOJO: They're not all of them bad, you know.

DANIELLE: You're a hundred years out of date, do you know that, Jojo?

JOJO: It's mothers brought them up, every man jack of them.

DANIELLE: You're obsolete!

LEILA: **(to DANIELLE)** Hey, hey, leave it, will you?

DANIELLE: **(over this, to JOJO)** Where the hell have you been?

JOJO: Right here. Working. I never close! Yeah, they broke the mould after me, eh?

DANIELLE: You're a bloody cliché, you know that, don't you?

JOJO: **(picking up her bottle, trying to remember how much she's had)** Guys ask for me. I can't be so dusty, if they still ask for –

DANIELLE: **(grabbing the bottle off JOJO)** For Crissake! It's breakfast time!

LEILA: **(grabbing the bottle from Danielle, To JOJO, gently)** Keep the rest for later, Jojo.

JOJO: Breakfast! Haven't seen a breakfast in years.

DANIELLE: Lucky you! Mornings are all I've got. Feed the kids, dress them, play with them . . . take them round the babysitter's, then snatch a few hours kip. There's no phone here. Do you think I could ask the Father to phone my childminder?

JOJO: Of course you could. He let Denise phone yesterday.

LEILA: He doesn't want to get involved, Father Gaillac. He kept well out the way during the Press conference. He sat at the back of the choir stalls. He was listening all right – but he never looked up.

DANIELLE: I'm worried sick about the kids.

LEILA: Moreau's the best minder you've ever had. She loves those kids of yours almost as much as she loves her own.

DANIELLE: Sure she does. But she does it for the money.

LEILA: We all do it for the money.

DANIELLE: Christ! What if I go to jail? How will I keep paying her? Non-payment of fines! This time I'm bound to go to jail. What if they take the kids away? They'll hate it – they'll – . . . What if I can't get them back?

LEILA: That's why we're here, remember –

DANIELLE: I'm worried sick.

LEILA: – because we're mothers, we're citizens. They're beginning to see that – things are changing already. Look at the food they bring us every day; blankets, newspapers, magazines. And the crowd outside – not just cops and journalists – students, housewives, factory-workers –

THERESE: And johns!

She and BRIGITTE giggle, imitate the punters.

THERESE: – hanging about out there – gasping for it –

BRIGITTE: Dying for it!

THERESE: – with their – tongues! – hanging out!

JOJO laughs with them. LEILA irritated by them.

LEILA: They're all talking about us, Danielle. Talking – not joking. That journalist – the one who came from Paris – he didn't stare us up and down. He's not going to write about tits and bums and turning tricks.

JOJO: Paris! I'm gonna get there, one of these days. Or Amsterdam maybe: one of those red-lit rooms in Amsterdam where you sit in the warm, in the window, and wave to the clients.

DANIELLE: Soon as I can I'm getting out of all this. Soon as I've paid off my debts, before the kids get older.

LEILA: Yes! Got to shape up before the kids get older . . .

THERESE: I'm going to be a policewoman, eventually. Or a screw.

LEILA: First of all the money: get the money, keep the money, hide it, bank it, feed it.

A sigh of recognition from the others, a pause.

DANIELLE: **(quietly, more resigned than scornful)** 'Darling!' Jesus – who do they think they are? 'Get 'em off, darling!' Who in hell do they think they are?

Scene 7

Outside the church.

INSPECTOR: A few names. That's all I'm asking for.

FATHER: If I knew, Inspector, I still couldn't tell you.

INSPECTOR: So the Church is taking sides.

FATHER: God's House belongs to everyone.

INSPECTOR: But the girls are vetting everyone who goes in and out. They're calling the shots! What does the Bishop say about that?

FATHER: The Bishop is in retreat.

INSPECTOR: Nice one! A sudden decision, was it? Look, all I want is confirmation of the ringleaders' names. Juliette What's Her Face, Denise Thing-me, Danielle the Cop Hater. The chief criminals.

FATHER: Criminals?

INSPECTOR: Soliciting, drugs, drink, theft, assault, breach of the peace, keeping a brothel. Then there's 'aiding and abetting'. Don't play the innocent, Father. There's a tide of seriously criminal scum all round your church. That boys' club you run – crime school, we call it. Didn't you know? Those kids don't stand a chance in hell – their mothers' being what they are.

FATHER: And the fathers?

INSPECTOR: There aren't any fathers. Only pimps.

FATHER: That isn't true.

INSPECTOR: Any man living with one of these women is a pimp.

FATHER: No. Not true.

INSPECTOR: The law says 'yes'. It's my job to clean the streets.

FATHER: That's what the killer says. In his phone calls to the press.

INSPECTOR: We're with him on that one. You don't watch them trade their filth night after night, Father Gaillac, you don't have to hunt them.

FATHER: Hunt them!

INSPECTOR: I suppose the Church regards them as a necessary evil. A safety valve? **(Stares at the Father speculatively.)** sure, okay, so we all do, right? But there are limits: sewers stink – they should be kept underground. **(No longer hiding his anger.)** The longer it takes – the worse it'll be – for them. You tell them, Father! Time to pack it in! You tell them – right?

FATHER GAILLAC goes into the church. (He remains onstage, occupied in some way – not in the chapel space, and not deliberately eavesdropping, but aware of the girls nearby and of their talk.)

Scene 8

JOJO is dolling herself up. LEILA comes on.

LEILA: What's all this? **(Or doesn't say it – just looks it.)**

JOJO: The mothers are here. They want to talk to us – no! No. They want us to talk to them! They're meeting at the West Door. They've brought 'refreshments'! How do I look?

LEILA surveys her.

JOJO: Like a mother?

LEILA hesitates.

JOJO: Like a pro, eh?

LEILA: They're only a bunch of mothers, Jojo, for god's sake.

JOJO: Motherhood's sacred, pet. The good sisters always used to tell us that.

LEILA: You're a mother, Jojo. We all are – except for Therese. Even Brigitte's going to be one, God help her.

JOJO: We're a bit different, though.

LEILA: We're not different! That's what we're protesting about.

JOJO: **(ignoring this – because she knows it isn't true; still dolling herself up for the meeting)** I love johns in skirts.

LEILA: What?

JOJO: I don't get many – but – you know – they're always so polite.

LEILA: The pervs usually are – beforehand.

JOJO: No – I mean the priests – the frocks. Mind you, they never come in their frocks. **(Suddenly, realising the innuendo, she gives a big, dirty laugh.)**

LEILA: **(irritated)** Oh, for Crissake!.

JOJO: **(thoughtfully)** Father's Gaillac's a lovely man, isn't he?

LEILA: **(really stern)** Don't even think about it.

JOJO: Now, would I? Would I?

LEILA: Just don't. Okay?

JOJO: The shy ones always choose me. I tell them: you should find a nice little girl-friend.

LEILA: They don't want 'nice'. They want dirt.

JOJO: Oh, you, you sound like Danielle. Some of them just want their mama.

LEILA: Which ones, though? It's hard to tell. The bloke who pulls a knife on you usually wears a suit and tie.

JOJO: I never have any trouble with my clients.

LEILA: Bollocks.

JOJO: No – I swear –

LEILA: **(cutting in)** You've been off work for days after –

JOJO: **(cutting in)** Apart from the odd nutter.

LEILA: There's an odd nutter out on the streets right now – with a hammer and a screwdriver –

JOJO: **(crosses herself quickly, determined to ignore the gory realities, brightly)** Are you coming to meet the mothers?

LEILA: I'll be along in a minute.

JOJO: Oh, come on, Leila. Come and 'partake of refreshments'.

LEILA: Vichy water and madeleines!

JOJO: No, no, it's good stuff. One of them's married to the bloke who runs the Hotel Leopold.

LEILA: **(laughs)** What? Well, he can afford a few sponge cakes!

JOJO: Of course he can!

LEILA: He makes more out of his call girls than the whole bloody police department makes out of us street-walkers.

JOJO: **(who didn't know this herself)** His wife wouldn't know about that!

LEILA: The rich ones with wedding rings – they're the biggest whores.

Some applause heard offstage – from the meeting.

JOJO: Aw, come on, Leila. A campaign, you said this was. Not a rest, you said.

LEILA: In a moment. Maybe.

JOJO: **(is leaving, but anxious for a last approval)** How do I look?

LEILA: You look really good, doll. **(Gives her a hug.)** Sock it to 'em from me, okay?

JOJO trips out. LEILA has become aware of FATHER GAILLAC's presence. She's unfazed by the possibility that he's heard some or all of the conversation. She is much easier with him than he with her.

LEILA: You should go to the meeting, Father. Hear what the girls have to say.

FATHER GAILLAC: Don't you think I might be one 'frock' too many? And you – aren't you going?

LEILA: I have to put on my armour first.

FATHER GAILLAC: You're going into battle?

LEILA: Would you meet the mothers in civvies? Jeans and t-shirt? You wear a disguise.

FATHER GAILLAC: No, no. these mark me as God's servant.

LEILA: You're invisible.

FATHER GAILLAC: Well, I hope not.

LEILA: When I work on the street, I'm invisible. **(She's forcing him to meet her gaze, to understand what she does, what it means.)** Just my clothes, just my body. I'm not there, not really. You can understand that?

FATHER GAILLAC: **(not wanting to)** I can try.

LEILA: Two or three hours later I can't remember what they looked like. It's like taking confession.

FATHER GAILLAC: **(shocked)** No, my child – it's not at all –

LEILA: **(in over this)** Leila.

FATHER GAILLAC: Leila. Leila, confession is about sorrow, expressing sorrow, and accepting forgiveness. A cleansing of the spirit.

LEILA: That's it exactly. That's why they pay. To hand over the sin. To hate the sinner.

They are still facing each other. Then she turns and moves away – to check her appearance with a small mirror, or makeup bag, adjust her skirt or ear-rings. She is donning her disguise, draping a jacket or jersey over one shoulder. She grows more distant, more daunting. He watches the transformation, watches as she goes. Then he goes to the confessional.

Scene 9

After the meeting. Two MOTHERS, each with a baby, in pouches slung across their chests, or just as shawled bundles.

FIRST MOTHER: Mothers! That's rich!

SECOND MOTHER: They do have kids, most of them.

FIRST MOTHER: Then why aren't they at home, looking after them? I feel – grubby! Did you hear that little skinny one say she was living rough?

SECOND MOTHER: They aren't very particular, are they?

FIRST MOTHER: No!

SECOND MOTHER: The men, I mean.

FIRST MOTHER snorts with contempt.

All sorts, they said: blue collar, white collar, young, old, rich, poor. **(Thoughtful.)** Ten or twelve tricks a night.

FIRST MOTHER: **(determined to ignore this, talks to her baby)** Who's waking up, then, eh? Who's waking up? Oh, you've been a good girl! Sleeping all through that meeting!

SECOND MOTHER: Five or six nights a week. Suppose each girl does sixty men a week . . .

FIRST MOTHER: **(to baby)** Who's ready to collect her big brother from school, then?

SECOND MOTHER: Or even only fifty. Each.

FIRST MOTHER: **(to baby)** Where's Jean-Claude, then? Where's that big brother of yours? **(To second mother.)** I'll have to hurry, or Jean-Claude'll get in a state. He needs his mummy terribly after a long day at school.

SECOND MOTHER: **(still doggedly calculating)** Say seven hundred prostitutes in the whole city. Then that's fifty times – at a conservative guess –

FIRST MOTHER: I don't want to know. I don't know any man that would. I don't know any man –

FIRST MOTHER goes.

SECOND MOTHER: That's thirty-five thousand 'tricks' a week. That's an awful lot of men. . . . Maybe not quite so many – maybe sometimes it's the same man goes twice – three times? – a week? **(Shocked, astonished, for a moment almost amused. Tenderly she strokes the baby's head.)** Maybe – even – sometimes . . . Daddy? **(Not amused now.)**

Scene 10

At the confessional.

The HOUSEWIFE could be the Second Housewife from the previous scene, or another.

HOUSEWIFE: Bless me, Father, for I have sinned. It is two weeks since I made my confession. I have not written to my sister in New Caledonia, I am jealous of her life in New Caledonia.

FATHER: Is this your only sin, my child?

HOUSEWIFE: I have not loved my neighbour. I let her clothes fall from the washing line. Her peach silk petticoat. It fell into the street below.

FATHER: Are these your only sins?

HOUSEWIFE: I have had lustful thoughts. For these and all my other sins I am very sorry.

FATHER: Say two Hail Marys and a Glory be to the Father, my child. **(He murmurs the absolution:)** God the Father of Mercies, through the death and resurrection of his Son, has reconciled the world to Himself and sent the Holy Spirit among us for the forgiveness of sins; through the ministry of the Church may God give you pardon and peace, and I absolve you from your sins in the name of the Father, and of the Son, and of the Holy Spirit.

During the FATHER's absolution, the HOUSEWIFE moves or turns away from the confessional. This part of her confession is between herself and her conscience only. As soon as she speaks, FATHER GAILLAC's absolution dies away.

HOUSEWIFE:
In my husband's bakery, I serve behind the counter.
Mother, wife, shop girl, busy, respectable.
I serve bread to a young man, the sunlight on his hair,
I want to run my hand through the gold flecks in his hair.
I think – **(She stops.)** – I want – **(Stops.)** I'm tired, so tired –
(. . .) I think of myself in a peach silk petticoat,
I feel my flesh fill out the silk of the petticoat,
I'm tired of being too tired, of baby milk and washing,
Baker's yeast and sour dough.
I want to be a wild rose, black bra, perfume,
White flesh, soft flesh.
I want to walk down Zola Street,
Vamp down Zola Street,
Fuck on Zo –

She stops – shocked at herself. Then collects herself, pulls up

her collar, checks her top button – 'dons her disguise' – stands demure, for her Hail Mary.

Hail Mary, full of Grace, the Lord is with you; blessed are you among women, and blessed is the fruit of your womb, Jesus. Holy Mary, Mother of God – . . .

During the HOUSEWIFE's Hail Mary, the MAN CONFESSING comes to the confessional. As soon as he speaks, the HOUSEWIFE's words fade to silence, she steps into the shadows of the church, and offstage.

MAN: Bless me, Father, for I have sinned. It's two months since I've made confession. I have lied, Father, I lied to the wife. Cars, that's my downfall – I bought a new Peugeot, I have got into debt with my new silver Peugeot, I drive the long way home, a detour through the city – dark streets, bright lights –

FATHER: Are these your only sins, my son?

MAN: Adultery, Father. I went with a whore.

FATHER: How many times my son?

MAN: Just the Friday. Last Friday.

FATHER: That is a mortal sin, my son. You should be careful on Fridays, you should drive straight home. Take the short route home on Fridays; drive calmly, think about your family, think about the weekend. Make your next Holy Communion part of your penance, my son. **(Continues, hurriedly, with the absolution.)** May God the Father of mercies, through the death, and resurrection of his son –

The MAN has turned, or stepped forward, speaking to his conscience. As soon as he speaks FATHER GAILLAC falls silent.

MAN:

Most Fridays. . . . Every Friday.
See, the traffic's bad that time of the week,
So the wife understands if I stop for a beer.
She's happy on Fridays, the kids round the table,
Bread and wine on the table.
I drive down Zola Street, up and down Zola Street.
The Cafe Cockatoo, it's close by Zola Street.
There's a woman there – she knows what I want –
Sweet scent, soft skin. I don't feel ashamed.
At least, not til after, when I make love to the wife.
When I make love to the wife, I sometimes think about the whore.
And yet, when I've paid the whore – when I've done the business –
Well, I'm dying to get home to the wife,
I can't wait to make up to the wife.

JOJO has approached the confessional. The MAN leaves as she starts to speak.

JOJO: Bless me, Father, for I have sinned. It's – oh, two months since I've made my confession.

Her opening words were formal, but the rest is less and less so. She is absolutely at ease; for her confession truly equals forgiveness, contact with Jesus, Mary – and FATHER GAILLAC. FATHER GAILLAC isn't so relaxed.

The thing is. I've been in court such a lot – it takes up so much time – even getting there, right the other side of town. These guys in court – you know, they get paid just hanging around waiting for things to start. Well – that's just what they've booked me for – hanging around waiting to work. And as soon as you're out of court, you've to work twice as hard just to pay off the fines. Cops, court, fines, streets; cops, court, fines, streets.

FATHER GAILLAC coughs warningly. JOJO doesn't take the hint.

Talk about conveyer belts –

FATHER GAILLAC: **(interrupting)** What are your sins, my child?

JOJO: Well . . . there's bad language, Father. I do try, I try and try. But now and again, the bad words just slip out.

FATHER GAILLAC: You must try harder, my child.

JOJO: What I wanted to tell you, Father: I've had to sell this ring. But it's not mine, see. It belonged to a client. He left it behind – oh, three, four months ago. They do that, they take off rings and watches, anything 'family' – it makes them –

FATHER GAILLAC: The ring, my child, the ring?

JOJO: He'd been a regular of mine. But after that night he never came back. If I'd taken it to the police, I mean, they'd have called me a thief. And suppose they'd found it round at my place? That would have –

FATHER GAILLAC: So you sold it? And what happened to the money?

JOJO: The money! Ah, the money! What happens to money, Father? What happens to money? They say it's the root of all evil. Is that in the bible? But anyway, that's wrong! No, let me tell you, it's not having money that leads to evil.

FATHER GAILLAC: Are these your only sins, my child?

JOJO: Yes, Father.

FATHER GAILLAC: You must be more –

JOJO: By rights, I should have been able to take it to the cops. I could have claimed it back by now. Except that some of the cops down there – not all, I'm not saying that – but there's one or two –

FATHER GAILLAC: **(stops himself just in time from calling her by name; embarrassed, has never encouraged chatty confessions)** Jo – My child: just make sure in future your visitors don't leave things behind.

JOJO: Oh, well – easy said, Father, easy said! The things I find, you wouldn't believe: keys, credit cards, underpants –

FATHER GAILLAC: **(cutting in hastily)** Four Hail Marys.

JOJO: For these and all my other sins, I'm very sorry, Father.

JOJO steps forward, away from the confessional, speaking to herself now, or her conscience.

JOJO: He's got a nose for money, Maurice. He'd have found that ring, wherever I'd got it hid. The coffee jar, the cistern, the crack in the kitchen wall. I don't want trouble, I get enough of that on the street. He's all I've got now my daughter's moved away. That's the way things are. . . . Oh, a classy, classy ring. The initials were entwined. A nice, sweet man. That's why he used to come to me. He wouldn't have an affair, he's a good Catholic, very devout. He's in love with his wife. She's so beautiful, he said. Like a statue, a madonna. They don't talk much, he said. In bed he hardly dares to touch her. Well, sometimes that's the way things are!

Scene 11

Sounds offstage of a fight between and RAYMOND. Their insults overlap, are difficult to make out because of their physical struggling.

JOJO turns from her confession monologue straight into this scene.

THERESE: Bastard!

RAYMOND: Lay off me, bitch!

THERESE: Lay off? After what you've been –

RAYMOND: Scum!

THERESE: Pervert!

RAYMOND: Whore!

THERESE: Wanker!

RAYMOND: Whore!

DANIELLE, LEILA and BRIGITTE have come on, trying to locate the trouble. THERESE enters with RAYMOND held in a very professional arm-lock.

JOJO: Sweet Mother of God –

LEILA: –

BRIGITTE watches joyfully.

LEILA: Therese, for Crissake –

JOJO: You're in church.

DANIELLE: **(it's an order)** Drop him! D'you hear? Let him go! Now!

THERESE lets him free, but she and BRIGITTE stand over him, won't let him up from the ground. Now and again during the dialogue each aims a kick at him. Therese's kicks are quite vicious.

JOJO: What's going on?

RAYMOND: Dirty whores.

THERESE: Don't say you haven't noticed!

BRIGITTE: Spying in the toilets. Brushing up against us.

THERESE: Creeping around at night when we're asleep.

BRIGITTE: Always brushing up against us.

THERESE: Stealing undies.

RAYMOND: Undies? You don't wear undies –

THERESE and BRIGITTE kick him. The others remonstrate with them.

RAYMOND: I'll report this.

THERESE: I'll report this. This time – and the other times. All the other times. The times you wouldn't pay.

LEILA: **(shocked)** Not here? In the church?

DANIELLE: **(in over LEILA's words)** You slut. **(Gives a violent shove.)** You slut!

THERESE: **(returning the shove)** Not here – before, in Zola Street. So smarmy – till after –

RAYMOND: You're not worth paying for.

THERESE: You're not worth –

JOJO: Enough!

DANIELLE: Shut it, okay?

RAYMOND: She took my wallet.

THERESE: You wouldn't pay.

RAYMOND: Changed my mind.

THERESE: You couldn't do it.

BRIGITTE: **(suddenly bold)** Couldn't do it. Couldn't get it up.

RAYMOND: Flaunting!

THERESE: **(standing belligerantly, bawdily, over him; flashing her breasts or flicking her skirt)** I've got things to flaunt, me!

He gets up, limps off. A silence as they watch him go. BRIGITTE's delight is obvious.

THERESE: **(unaware of the menace in her stance, voice)** I used to be an angel. I was an angel when I was a kid.

Without realising she's doing it, she's cracking her knuckles.

DANIELLE: This is a church –

THERESE gives her a V sign.

Okay, he's a creep.

THERESE: Scum.

DANIELLE: We're seeking sanctuary here –

BRIGITTE: It's not his church.

THERESE: It was his fault – his! He's the one –

DANIELLE: All right, all right, we know, we know.

LEILA: We're trying to get respect, for Crissake –

JOJO: All this language!

LEILA: That's why we're here. But it works both ways – you've got to give respect, too.

THERESE: To that? That slime-bag!

LEILA: Well, no. Well – yes, I mean, you've got to –

THERESE gives her a V sign.

JOJO: Don't do that in here.

THERESE does it again.

JOJO: That's bad, girl. Really bad. I'm not staying for any more of this.

JOJO is going. She turns back in time to see THERESE aiming another V sign at her.

THERESE: **(muttering)** In front of Our Lady, too. You ought to be ashamed.

DANIELLE: **(to THERESE)** Look, the girls from the nylon factories, and the guys from the car line, and the students and the housewives: they trip over your bedding when they come to mass. They can't use the toilets, we've taken them over. The whole place stinks of bean and garlic stew. And no-one's complained –

THERESE: Why should they? They don't have to sleep here -

LEILA: Don't pick fights.

THERESE: I didn't.

DANIELLE: Don't stir it –

THERESE: I don't.

LEILA: And don't mock JOJO.

THERESE gives another V sign and walks off.

LEILA: **(to DANIELLE)** Don't you mock JOJO either, okay?

DANIELLE: What's up with you?

LEILA: You want respect? Well, give JOJO respect, okay?

DANIELLE: I'd give her the shirt off my back – I have done, many times. Okay?

LEILA: Don't call her a cliché.

DANIELLE: Oh, for Crissake!

LEILA: We're all getting older.

DANIELLE: My God, that's profound. What's that supposed to mean?

LEILA: We're all in the same boat.

DANIELLE: speak for yourself. Some of us have kids to look after. **(Regrets this remark immediately.)** Anyway, I look out for Jojo.

LEILA: Don't call her a fucking cliché, okay?

DANIELLE: You're a real cow when you haven't had a fix, Leila.

LEILA: I don't do that stuff anymore.

DANIELLE: No? You buy it –

LEILA: – for Bernard.

DANIELLE: Oh, come on!

LEILA: I hardly use it.

DANIELLE: Well, you can't, not in here.

LEILA: I can take it or leave it.

DANIELLE: Better leave it, then, Leila.

DANIELLE lights a fag – sees LEILA's hungry face – passes it to her. A pause.

BRIGITTE: **(to LEILA)** You've not got any kids, then?

DANIELLE: Sure, she's got kids. We all have – except THERESE. You should go back home now, Brigitte. That baby of yours needs a home.

BRIGITTE: I'm not giving up my baby.

DANIELLE: That's not what I'm saying. I said –

BRIGITTE: I'll give it a home. I'll make sure we have a home.

LEILA: They'll probably take it away. The social, the cops – even your own family can steal away your kids. You hardly know it's happening.

DANIELLE: **(to BRIGITTE)** Where are you staying?

BRIGITTE: I'm saving up.

LEILA: So am I. Saving up. Paying off all the fines, all the debts. I'll see my kids again, eventually.

BRIGITTE: Did you leave them?

DANIELLE: **(sharply)** No, of course she didn't. They're being well looked after.

LEILA: More than I was. I was just a piece of furniture.

DANIELLE: You're a piece of furniture now, doll. Bernard's furniture.

LEILA: You're a manhater, Danielle. Just because you aren't lucky in love.

DANIELLE: Love! Screwing is screwing. . . . And pimping is pimping.

LEILA: **(sings)** She can't get no – satisfaction . . . da,da,da,da – satisfaction. . .

DANIELLE: Once in a blue moon.

LEILA stops singing. She and BRIGITTE exchange glances.

Once or twice. An accident. Not with one of God's gifts, funnily enough. No – it'd be a short, fat guy with a beer belly. Well, clean enough, he'd have to be, I don't do them if they aren't. But the kind of guy who smells of his work, the kind of smell he can't scrub away. Newsprint, or diesel – or chickens – or pigs. . .

They laugh.

LEILA: Charge them extra, do you?

DANIELLE: You think I'd let them know?

LEILA: It's worth more than a hundred.

DANIELLE: What kind of slut to do you take me for?

LEILA: A lousy hundred. Jesus! If I wasn't on the streets – if I was working the Hotel Leopold – I could make five hundred – eight!

DANIELLE: Go on, then, get on with it.

LEILA: Think I couldn't? Think we all belong in the gutter, do you?

DANIELLE: I'm not in the gutter.

LEILA: Well, I'm not.

They both feel unsure. BRIGITTE's aware of their anxiety.

LEILA: **(to BRIGITTE)** What do you think, kid? Is this the gutter?

DANIELLE: **(to BRIGITTE, seriously)** How do you think you're going to manage with this baby, when it arrives?

BRIGITTE: You manage okay.

DANIELLE: Oh, sure. Motherhood is sacred, right? And the Mother of Mothers intercedes for us up above.

BRIGITTE: 'Her eyes are large. They see all our needs; her mouth is small, symbolising the fewness of her words.'

DANIELLE: Then it's high time she opened that mouth of hers wide –

LEILA: **(singing)** *Hail Mary, full of grace, the Lord is with thee –*

DANIELLE: **(over this)** – and gave a loud shout!

LEILA: **(singing)** *Maria Magdalena –*

She beefs up the rhythm slightly. LEILA and BRIGITTE are joining in.

DANIELLE:

Maria gives you what you want
And knows exactly what you are.

BRIGITTE: *Maria Magdalena*!

LEILA: **(chanting)** *She and her sisters are searched and fined and registered common in writing.*

BRIGITTE and DANIELLE: *Maria Magdalena!*

LEILA:
If men were hunted in darkness in the streets
If men were searched and registered common in writing!

All three, in turn, are moving/dancing to the rhythm.

The politician,
The country hick,
The curious student,
The business man with his suit and tie and nasty habits,
The sad man no-one loves –
Have mercy on them, O Lord,
We will love them,
In a manner of speaking,
In a manner of fucking

FATHER GAILLAC enter, with RAYMOND and JOJO.

Lord, you made us what men need,
We are the servants of the Lord.
Maria Magdalena Judith Jezebel Salome,
Maria Magdalena Judith Jezebel Salome,
Bad girl, big mouth, good time –

Seeing FATHER GAILLAC they stop abruptly. Only BRIGITTE, unaware of them, continues a bit longer, dancing and singing.

FATHER GAILLAC: There's been a telephone message for Mademoiselle Marteau.

DANIELLE: **(immediate panic)** The kids. They've taken the kids.

JOJO: No – no –

FATHER GAILLAC: The little boy is sick.

DANIELLE already moving to where her things are, stuffing them in her bag.

THE OTHERS: Danielle – Wait – Hold on –

JOJO: He's being looked after, he's in hospital. It's the croup.

DANIELLE determined to go.

LEILA: Wait, hold on Danielle, wait.

JOJO: Wait, Danielle, wait a minute, you can't go.

DANIELLE: **(to FATHER GAILLAC)** Where is he? Which hospital?

RAYMOND: St. Luke's.

THE OTHERS: **(trying to prevent DANIELLE going)** Wait. 'No-one leaves!' Remember? 'No-one leaves!'

DANIELLE: Are you deaf? He's sick. Pierrot's sick.

THERESE has come in, she stands watching this.

LEILA: 'No-one leaves!'

DANIELLE: What do you take me for?

LEILA: **(shouting)** They'll arrest you!

DANIELLE: Let them try!

FATHER GAILLAC, and RAYMOND, are on the edge of this, ignored.

FATHER GAILLAC: Let's have some calm. Let's all calm down.

They ignore him.

DANIELLE: **(pushing the restraining women away)** Get off. Fuck off.

FATHER GAILLAC: At least hear the message.

THERESE: **(her words are heard very clearly, a strong warning)** It's a trick.

RAYMOND: **(to THERESE)** No, it's not. They phoned.

THERESE: **(again, a strong note of warning)** It's a con!

RAYMOND: They said the little boy had croup, but it was under control, they said, he was fine. And you can visit any time. Any time, day or night.

THERESE: 'Visit any time'! It's a trick!

RAYMOND: Why would I lie – about a kid?

THERESE: It's the cops!

DANIELLE: **(muttering, frantic)** Shut up, shut up, for Crissake, shut up, shut up.

LEILA: What about Madame Moreau? What about the child-minder – was it her on the phone?

RAYMOND: A hospital person. I don't know.

THERESE: Trick or not, they'll book you the second you step outside.

DANIELLE: I've got to go, okay? I've got to.

They all start on at DANIELLE again, in a babble:

They'll throw you in the cells –
You'll never see Pierrot –
They'll be right outside –
You'll never get near the hospital –

DANIELLE: He nearly died of croup once, he gets it real bad.

FATHER GAILLAC: **(what else can he say)** I'm sure he's being well looked after.

DANIELLE: What do you know? What do you know about kids? **(Indicates the Madonna and Child.)** You think they're all like him? **(FATHER GAILLAC tries to protest – he's helped plenty families in sickness and death – but she won't let him.)** You think I can't look after him because I'm a whore? Is that it? You think I got my kids from some jerk who paid the going rate? Well, what if I did? I bore them, they're mine! They tried to take him off me as soon as he was born. Those bloody penguins! They put the pen in my hand. 'Sign this, my child, it's just medicine for the baby'! They kept pushing the pen into my hand. I signed nothing – I signed nothing! Nothing, nothing!

JOJO: Come on now, darling, they won't take Pierrot. They wouldn't dare.

LEILA: The Press wouldn't stand for it.

JOJO: Sure, you wouldn't stand for it, would you, Father?

He's silent, feels useless.

DANIELLE: They'll ask questions at the hospital. They'll take the kids away. **(The others are around her, wanting to comfort her.)** The very same jerks who want a screw in the back of the car – they'll sit in court in the morning – and sign my kids away.

Act 2

Scene 1

Night.

Offstage: A stick, or iron bar, is run menacingly along a fence, railings, or corrugated iron – and back again.

EXCITED MAN: Ripper eight – police nil! Ripper eight – police nil!

All the speeches are delivered very fast:

FAMILY VALUES MAN: These women lead the men astray. They spread disease, you don't know where they've been, they live like rats. They make me sick. They see five men a day – eight men – ten. Good God, they've got kids, they get pregnant! It makes me sick, I don't want to think about it. Suppose my wife should think about it? I've got three daughters, a very happy home. I don't know any man who does it, these men are led astray. I don't know any man – there aren't that many, I don't know any man! These women should be locked away, adultery, that's what it is, breaking up the happy home. Back in the box, right? Back in the sink, out of sight, off the street, steralise them, throw away the key, throw away the key. . .

VICIOUS WOMAN: Ripper eight – police nil. Takes a real bloody butcher to keep them off the streets. And about time too. Oh, it's not just the whores – they can look after themselves – but what about the other slags, what about the feminists, eh? Students? Social workers? Women's lib? They're all tarts, paid or unpaid: out all hours, dressed like dogs' dinners, dressed like dogs' dinners. Trying to live like men: drugs, drink, sex, the pill! Well, they're shit scared now, eh? Run for a bus now, eh? Jump in a taxi now? Serve em right, shit scared, off the street, back in the kitchen, back with the kids, back in the sink, back in the box. . . **(Laughs malevolently.)**

EXCITED MAN: Two weeks in church! Two weeks in church with nothing but women! They'll be dying for it when they get out! Dying for it! Two weeks! Dying for it – I am – dying for it – I am. What I wouldn't give! **(Growls or roars.)** Come out, come out whoever you are, eh? I'm not fussy! Murder for it, I would, oh, yes, no lie. Kill for it, I would, kill for it, murder for it. . .

Offstage. The stick or bar runs along the fence again.

VARIOUS VOICES:

Ever-y-bod-y-on-the-streets!
Hor-i-zon-tal!
Ever-y-bod-y-on-the-streets!
Hor-i-zon-tal!
Ready or no-o-o-ot!
Puss, puss, puss, puss,

Whap! – A dustbin lid clangs – or the stick/bar clangs along the railings.

Ready or no-o-o-ot!
Pussy in the chuuuurch!
Pussy in the chuuuurch!

Offstage. The stick runs along the fence again. Motorcycles roaring, circling the church area.

Scene 2

Before the noise from the previous scene has died away, THERESE and BRIGITTE come on, with Danielle's baby.

BRIGITTE: There's more of them out there than last night.

THERESE: Maybe they just shout louder.

BRIGITTE settling the baby.

THERESE: Looking forward to it, then? Eh? Motherhood!

BRIGITTE: Sure.

THERESE: Going to work with a pram in tow, are you?

BRIGITTE: Danielle gets by.

THERESE: She never has any fun, though.

BRIGITTE: You have fun, do you?

THERESE: **(cracking her knuckles)** Who says I don't?

BRIGITTE: **(after a pause, feeling her way carefully)** You got a place of your own?

THERESE: A room? Yeah, I got a room. . . . I'll get a swimming pool, eventually.

BRIGITTE: I don't suppose –

THERESE: No.

BRIGITTE: I'd pay my share, it's just for a bit –

THERESE: Jesus, you're green! We'd get done, cretin! Two of us living together? That's a brothel. We'd get jail! Even if we worked out in the car park, and only came home to sleep and eat. Didn't anyone tell you? That's why nobody's offered to take you in. . . . We'll find you something, don't worry. There's rooms – if you can pay.

BRIGITTE: I've got fines to pay already.

THERESE: You shouldn't work your ass off all the time, you know. Try a bit of thieving. When they're busy with the sex – when their brains are in their balls – that's when you pinch the wallet –

BRIGITTE: They'd batter you – surely –

THERESE: Well, you don't thieve on your own patch! Not unless he's blind drunk. But maybe in his car – when he's pulling up his pants, say you need a pee, and scarper.

BRIGITTE: But if you met him again –

THERESE: The dopes are easy to spot, they stick out a mile.

BRIGITTE not convinced.

THERESE: Well, if you don't fancy rolling them – clip them instead. Outside the hotels. Take the money, and tell him you'll book the room – they don't like showing their faces at the desk – then run in the hotel, and straight out the back. Toilets or kitchens. Make sure you check it out before, though. Or if you're on a high, just run, soon as he gives you the dosh. I get a real buzz from that – I know the alleys like the back of my hand, I can always get away – and if I didn't – **(She flicks open her knife, nonchalantly.)**

LEILA and JOJO come on.

LEILA: Hey, what rubbish are you filling that child's head with now?

THERESE turns to her, brandishing the knife, more mischievous than menacing.

LEILA: **(unimpressed)** Oh, put that away.

JOJO: Don't listen to a word she says, Brigitte.

THERESE: I'm telling her the score, why not?

JOJO: No bad advice, now. **(To BRIGITTE.)** Don't try any rolling or clipping, okay?

LEILA: **(to THERESE)** You're the kind gives tarts a bad name.

THERESE: I make more dosh than either of you.

LEILA: Oh, yes – and what do you do with it?

THERESE: I don't get it ponced off me, that's for sure.

JOJO: What do you mean, ponce? You calling Maurice a ponce?

THERESE: **(to JOJO)** Where is all your dosh? **(To LEILA.)** Eh?

LEILA: Where's yours?

BRIGITTE: She has fun. She has fun with her dosh.

THERESE: **(still has the knife out, to BRIGITTE)** Shut it, you!

LEILA: Oh, put that away, silly bitch. This is no place for fights.

THERESE: Oh, dearie goodness me, I forgot, we're in church! Hail Mary, full of shit. Healers, and hostesses and sisters of mercy. And all the clients are lovely, all the regulars are really nice, and the pimps are so sweet, they'd give you the shirt off their backs –

LEILA about to shove her or swipe at her. Threatens her.

Speaking together:

JOJO: Aw, come on, doll, don't be that way.

LEILA: Any more of that, girl, you'll be out on your ear.

JOJO: **(about to put an arm round BRIGITTE)** Come on now, darling, put that away, come and have a drink.

But THERESE shrugs her off.

THERESE: **(to BRIGITTE)** You look after it, okay?

LEILA: Shut up, you're worse than the bloody cops!

LEILA goes off, with the baby.

JOJO: **(to LEILA, as she follows her out)** She's upset again. She gets upset.

THERESE: **(to BRIGITTE)** If you're going to keep that precious baby once it pops out your holy, holy, holy, you'd better bloody look out for it. Make sure everyone treats it right, all of them. You let anything happen to your kid – I'll have your guts.

BRIGITTE goes. RAYMOND in, cleaning.

RAYMOND: A good-looking wee fella, that baby.

THERESE: Keep clear of the baby, right?

RAYMOND: I'm only saying –

THERESE: Judas.

RAYMOND: I'm not. I never.

That phone message about the baby! In the hospital? Dying of the croup? It was a trick!

RAYMOND: I didn't know that, I didn't know.

THERESE: Shove off.

RAYMOND continues cleaning.

THERESE: Piss off! Okay?

He continues cleaning. She lifts her blouse/tank top, and flashes her bra at him.

THERESE: Okay?

RAYMOND: **(continues staring after the 'flash' is over, mesmerised, and shocked)** In church! No shame. No shame.

He turns away, continues cleaning.

THERESE: **(calls quietly – quite nicely – as if she's about to apologise)** Look, Raymond –

THERESE flashes again as RAYMOND turns.

THERESE: You looked!

RAYMOND: **(trying to tear his gaze away)** I never. No.

THERESE: **(takes the knife out again, examines it, already forgetting about RAYMOND)** I used to be an angel when I was a kid. I'm going to be a policewoman, eventually. Or a screw. I'm going to bang up all the pervs that muck up all the kids. I'll give them hell. Oh, yes. I will.

THERESE puts the knife away and goes.

Scene 3

JOJO in, fetches a stool, in order to reach the Madonna. Smiles a greeting to RAYMOND, and begins cleaning the Madonna.

RAYMOND: That's my job.

JOJO: You work here full-time, then, Raymond, do you?

RAYMOND: No. No, I don't.

JOJO: You're here all the time, though. (. . .) Aw, look – lipstick on Our Lady! That'll be Therese.

RAYMOND: That Therese – something wrong with that one.

JOJO: She gets upset.

RAYMOND: Broke my arm, just about. (. . .) I didn't not pay. I don't go with them – so why would I be paying?

JOJO: It's nothing to be ashamed of, Raymond.

RAYMOND: What?

JOJO: Paying for it.

RAYMOND: I don't.

JOJO: Aw, come on, you're always down Zola Street.

RAYMOND: I walk to work, what am I supposed to do, go the long way round? Why should I?

JOJO: It's a straight business transaction. You get what you pay for.

RAYMOND: **(in over this)** Me! I don't, no.

JOJO: Fair dos.

RAYMOND: If you get what you pay for.

JOJO: But, if you despise what you pay for – what does that make you?

RAYMOND: I don't

JOJO: **(kindly)** Aw, you're crazy for Zola street, just crazy for it.

RAYMOND: **(cutting in)** I'm not.

JOJO: You're not alone, son, there's loads of them, they all want it.

RAYMOND: **(softly, to himself)** Mystery. . .

JOJO: **(hasn't heard)** What?

RAYMOND: Soft skin –

JOJO: **(hasn't heard)** It's quite straightfor –

RAYMOND: No! It's not. It shouldn't be – not like that! It's wrong – disgusting!

JOJO: **(in over this)** If you pay –

RAYMOND: **(in over this)** I don't –

JOJO: **(in over this)** If you despise –

RAYMOND: **(in over this)** Anyway, I don't –

JOJO: Aw, son, come on –

RAYMOND: I don't know what you mean.

Stalemate.

JOJO: They're nice girls, ordinary girls.

RAYMOND: **(low)** Let you down. Take the piss.

JOJO: **(hasn't heard, runs on)** Well – not those slags down the fishmarket, you need to watch those junkies! But we're all of us daughters, sisters, mothers.

RAYMOND: My mother slaved for us. Worked in the mill, looked after us all at home. My old man – he showed my sister the door – when she stayed out late, started dressing like a tart. Kicked her out. Goodbye. 'She should have been the boy,' he said. 'Too much spirit. Should have been the boy. What have we got left? Kick the ball, Raymond. Kick the bloody ball, son.' 'Listen son, take my advice: if you're not in by ten – come home. Ha, ha. Get in there, son! In by ten, d'you hear me?'

JOJO: **(busy at the statue, not talking to him directly)** It's not wrong to pay, so long as you treat them nice.

RAYMOND: **(muttering)** In by ten! Like the old man upstairs, Friday nights, the big stick, the big stick.

JOJO: They've the right to stand there, if you've the right to look them over.

RAYMOND: I don't.

DANIELLE has come on. They don't notice.

JOJO: Where's the harm?

RAYMOND: It shouldn't be like that.

JOJO: You should ask for Cara. She's a nice quiet girl. Blond. No oil-painting, mind, but she has lots of regulars. She makes them feel good, she'll not throw you out in four minutes flat, like Danielle would.

RAYMOND: Cara? Hangs out in the Cockatoo? Short? Bandy legs?

DANIELLE: A pretty good bargain, wouldn't you say? For a guy with a paunch, and bad breath – not to mention what else he might –

JOJO: **(shouting over her)** Aw, shut up, who asked you to butt in?

RAYMOND retreats. JOJO upset for him, angry with DANIELLE.

DANIELLE: I'm no social worker.

JOJO: No.

DANIELLE: It's always someone else's fault! Sister, mother – even the whore's bloody fault! 'Coming on too strong!' 'Too quick!' Why can't they take their own blame? **(Grim amusement.)** Cara the blackleg! The only hooker left on the street. She must be coining it out there! Dumbcluck! Let's hope she stays alive long enough to bank the dosh.

LEILA in.

LEILA: They've doubled the guard on the church.

JOJO: On the doors?

LEILA: Not us, no – outside – the cops. They're putting a cordon round the church. Wall to wall cops.

JOJO: **(laughs)** What do they think we're going to do? Run away?

DANIELLE: Hunt the slags. Couldn't three or four of them go and play Hunt the Ripper for a while? Maybe even go and catch him?

LEILA: I'm surprised Father Gaillac allowed you to keep Pierrot here. It's not safe for a baby.

DANIELLE: Safer than outside.

LEILA: Why the hell couldn't you leave him with Madame Moreau?

DANIELLE: After the way those pigs messed about on the phone?

JOJO: He's a tonic, that baby, he never cries –

DANIELLE: **(cutting in, to LEILA.)** Look, they were at Madame Moreau twice a day, they never stopped grilling her –

LEILA: Well, she couldn't tell what she didn't know –

DANIELLE: **(cutting in)** They tried to say she's running a brothel. They threatened to take Pierrot and Suzanne and her own kids away, they said she'd never work as a childminder again –

LEILA: And what if the cops bust in here – what'll –

DANIELLE: **(who is worried about this too; cutting in)** Don't worry about my kids, Leila, I look after my kids!

LEILA: Listen, Wonderwoman, I never neglected –

DANIELLE: Oh, no?

LEILA: My kids have everything –

DANIELLE: Not their mother.

LEILA: I left them in (good hands) –

DANIELLE: **(in over this)** Left them – yes! Off to join the students in sixty-eight!*

LEILA: The best time of my life. I learned to live.

DANIELLE: And someone else learned to look after your kids.

* 'Sixty-eight': Student's revolution, which spread to several cities, including Paris.

LEILA: If we all stayed at home the world would never change! We'd never grow up!

JOJO: Oh, quit rowing, the pair of you. **(To DANIELLE.)** Give her a cigarette.

DANIELLE: Haven't got one.

JOJO: Father Gaillac gave you some, I know he did.

DANIELLE: She's already had a smoke with those junkies down the end of the nave.

LEILA: I was never out that house, four walls, that's all I ever saw. I needed to find out who I was.

DANIELLE: I found out who I was when my children were born.

LEILA: Well, I didn't, okay? I was young, good-looking. I wanted more, much more. Why not?

A silence. DANIELLE and JOJO stare at her. It's obvious she's got nothing. BRIGITTE is passing through with large coffee pot.

BRIGITTE: Grub up! Come and get it!

JOJO: Coming, doll. Just coming.

DANIELLE: Brigitte!

BRIGITTE: **(stops)** Um?

DANIELLE and JOJO look at LEILA. DANIELLE wants to say to BRIGITTE: 'Don't be like Leila here, for God's sake, go home, give yourself and your baby a chance.' But how to say it?

DANIELLE: **(to BRIGITTE)** Oh, nothing. Just coming.

BRIGITTE goes. DANIELLE and JOJO follow.

LEILA: **(quietly)** As much as I could get. Why not?

LEILA follows the others.

Scene 4

Outside on the street.

FATHER GAILLAC is on his way to the church, laden with supplies: large loaves, some wine, newspapers. The INSPECTOR hails him.

INSPECTOR: Well, if it isn't the padre! Off to feed the five thousand. How's the harem? Must be a hard grind! Keeping your end up?

FATHER GAILLAC: Good morning, Inspector. Any news of Genevieve?

INSPECTOR: **(barring his way)** Assaulting a police officer, are we?

FATHER GAILLAC: With an armful of loaves and fishes?

As the INSPECTOR takes a loaf from the FATHER, he knocks the other supplies to the ground. He breaks into the loaf.

INSPECTOR: Who'll feed the harem, if the padre's in the cooler?

FATHER GAILLAC: The Mothers' Union, the Press, the students, the factory workers –

INSPECTOR: They're cock-a-hoop, those slags, they really think they're something, don't they? Think they've a right to do as they please –

FATHER GAILLAC: They have no rights, Inspector, none at all. They are persecuted by the law, they are victims –

INSPECTOR: They will be! I warned you, didn't I? The longer it takes . . . But it won't take long.

FATHER GAILLAC: Look, isn't there some way – isn't there some –

INSPECTOR: (Cutting in, on top of this.) We won't be asking you for names anymore. We've got those. Two of my men have been to mass: officers from out of town, unknown faces. One of them even went to confession first! He had a good look round. The duty roster in the vestry was very helpful. We've got all the names we need. **(FATHER GAILLAC starts to pick up some of the fallen supplies.)** You've a baby in the church, I hear.

FATHER GAILLAC: That's right. He's only three months old, he needs his mother.

INSPECTOR: Social services will be wanting to look into that.

FATHER GAILLAC: St Joseph's is a sanctuary for any –

INSPECTOR: Sanctuary, my arse! We're not in the dark ages now. The state's in charge, not the Vatican. They're at it in Paris now – copycat slags – hundreds of them. Stopping the traffic. Bunging up the churches. Taking the piss. Threatening to name names. The President's been in touch with your superiors.

FATHER GAILLAC: These are my parishioners.

INSPECTOR: I'm standing by for orders. All we need is one excuse. . . . Confession must be quite an uplifting occasion these days? Sets the juices running, does it?

FATHER GAILLAC: People don't confess what they don't regard as sin.

INSPECTOR: Sounds clever. What's it mean?

FATHER GAILAC: Perhaps the clients have more to confess than the girls.

INSPECTOR: What do they confess?

FATHER GAILLAC: Penitents are never betrayed, inspector. You know that. Names are never named: no prostitute, politician, pervert, pimp . . . pig.

INSPECTOR goes. FATHER GAILLAC retrieves the rest of the supplies.

I listen to them all. Receive their sadness, eat their shit . . . forget their faces, ignore their names . . . I'm invisible. What they need is each other, not me. . . . I'm not there. . .

Scene 5

FATHER GAILLAC goes into the church. The women arrive, some of them with their coffee mugs, or croissants. With the exception of DANIELLE, they are all excited, the younger two jubilant even.

BRIGITTE: Solidarity, Father! The working girls of France have adopted our charter! Marseille, Nice, Lille, Grenoble –

The others say good morning more tactfully, aware of his embarrassement.

THERESE: The girls of Paris are on strike.

LEILA: We heard it on the radio. They've taken a church in every district –

BRIGITTE: St Cyr, Bois de Boulogne –

THERESE: St Denis, Pigalle –

BRIGITTE: Solidarity!

JOJO: Long live Paris!

BRIGITTE: That'll show the Minister for Female Affairs!

THERESE: And the Minister of the Interior!

DANIELLE: Something wrong, Father?

He pulls out the newspaper, hands it to her.

DANIELLE: **(reads)** 'Hookers Hog the House of God!'

JOJO: Well, that's not very nice, is it?

LEILA: **(reads)** 'Enough is Enough.' Jerome Barsalou! But he was one of the journalists who came to our meetings, he came to all the meetings.

DANIELLE: That was last week, though.

LEILA: '. . . if motherhood is so important to these women, why are they still in the church of St Joseph. . . ' Christ! His newspaper sent us flowers!

DANIELLE: On expenses.

THERESE: The baker used to send us croissants and rum babas.

DANIELLE: Last week. Last week.

JOJO: Remember that wine someone sent? Oh, that was grand stuff – the best I've ever tasted.

DANIELLE: Last week.

THERESE: It's only the newspapers that are against us!

JOJO: And the fuzz.

LEILA: And the government.

DANIELLE: And the punters. It's not just the odd pervert screaming abuse out there every night. It's our fellow citizens.

FATHER GAILLAC: You think some of them might be your, um, clients?

DANIELLE: You can bet on it, Father.

LEILA: There were mothers out there too. Housewives.

BRIGITTE: But the housewives support us.

DANIELLE: Last week.

BRIGITTE: Well, the Catholic Women Workers do. Denise gave their President copies of the charter, didn't she?

DANIELLE: Ten days ago, Brigitte.

LEILA: **(reading)** 'My city's plagued with prostitutes – '

THERESE: His city!

LEILA: **(reading)** ' – but I guarantee they'll all be gone, every one of them, by Christmas!'

JOJO: Who's that?

FATHER GAILLAC: The Vice Squad chief.

THERESE: His city!

DANIELLE: Bloody lovely, that is! From the man who buys in call girls for his buddies, and rents a suite in the Hotel Leopold –

JOJO: I never knew that!

DANIELLE: – dresses up in see-through chiffon, dances with Thomasina, Dick and Harry – especially Dick and Harry –

JOJO: He shouldn't be so down on us, then, should he? That's not fair!

DANIELLE: Bloody lovely!

JOJO: Do you think we're a plague, Father?

FATHER: No, Jojo, of course I don't.

THERESE: They're scum, though, aren't they, Father, the pigs?

FATHER: **(more to himself than the others)** 'A sea of scum all round the church.'

LEILA: What do you think, though, Father?

FATHER GAILLAC: I told you what I thought in my sermon on Sunday.

Blank looks. None of them actually listened to it.

BRIGITTE: Up there in the pulpit, you mean?

FATHER GAILLAC: You didn't hear it up there?

The silence says: well, no. RAYMOND has been hovering for a while, listening.

THERESE: **(not directly to FATHER GAILLAC)** A sermon! For Pete's sake!

But the others wait for him to speak. They are not in a tight, obvious group, but they are around him, ready to listen to him now. He doesn't feel awkward with them now, the only hesitation is occasionally searching for the right words.

FATHER GAILLAC: It isn't what I think, it's what I know. It's wrong. Prostitution is wrong. (. . .) But an awful lot of things are wrong, an awful lot of other things are far more wrong. The sea of filth all round us, the sea of scum all round this church: cruelty, poverty, venom, murder. When we should be marked by love. Christ marks our lives by love: each sacrament is like – each one brings – a sign of love, a physical sign. The host we eat, the wine we drink, the blessing of baptism, and of absolution. The most private act of all is the union between man and wife. Which is an act of love, a physical sign of love for each other, and love in Christ. And any other kind of union – well, it's wrong.

They are thoughtful.

JOJO: **(breaking the spell)** If only! Eh, Father? If only!

RAYMOND has gone. The women are moving away. Except for THERESE, who has her knife out, is jabbing with it, almost absently, at a pew/screen/pillar.

JOJO: **(going)** They want more than that, though, Father, far more!

LEILA: **(going)** As much as they can get!

Only THERESE remains, and FATHER GAILLAC. He watches her, vandalising his church with her knife. After a moment he goes to her, reaches out to touch her hand or arm to signal her to stop. For a second, not realising who it is, she reacts aggressively. He takes the knife. She's suddenly aware of the mess she's made.

THERESE: Did I do that? Jesus, sorry, Father!

FATHER GAILLAC: Do you really need to carry this?

THERESE: **(taking it back from him)** Yeah, I need it.

FATHER GAILLAC: Doesn't it make things more dangerous? Any punter could take it from you, he could use it against you.

THERESE: **(confident)** I know how to use a knife. I feel safer with a knife.

A pause. She sits with the knife, fiddling a bit. He sits. Vaguely he feels she might need to talk, so he waits.

THERESE: **(holding the knife up, squinting at it)** 'I'm the man – ' . . . 'I'm the man you love to hate!'

A silence. Once, twice, she is about to speak, then changes her mind. He waits.

THERESE: That's what he used to say. When he came for the rent. 'I'm the man you love to hate! Where's the rent? – Behind the clock!' Big joke. My mother used to laugh, my mum and my nan. Behind the clock. I only took one note – a fifty franc note – I wanted to buy stuff for my mates. I wanted them to be my mates. My mum was out, taking Nana to the doctor. 'Where's the rent? I'll tell your Mum. Where's the rent? I'll tell your Nan. You've got to pay me. I'm the man – ' (. . .) Dress all mucky. Made me all mucky. Afterwards, he pissed on me. (. . .) And the next Tuesday, and the next, and the next. Mum visiting the hospital, Nana in the hospital. So then . . . so then, I turn the gas on, right up full. He always had a fag, he smoked all the time. I wanted him to die. I thought we'd blow away, both of us. It didn't work out, though. The kitchen went on fire, but we were – we weren't in the kitchen. The only one that died was Nana, in the hospital. (. . .) I used to be an angel. I used to go to mass with Nana.

A pause. still fiddling with the knife. FATHER GAILLAC reaches out, gently takes it.

THERESE: Well, I don't go now. **(Kicking at something, fidgety.)** Confession, mass.

FATHER GAILLAC: I could hear your confession now, if you like.

THERESE: I don't do that shit anymore.

She reaches for her knife, but he won't let her have it.

FATHER GAILLAC: Yes, that's the word: shit. Sometimes I feel like a toilet: flushing away the shit.

She's listening.

FATHER GAILLAC: Sometimes. By and large though, confession makes me realise how good people are.

She's irritated – this sounds like 'sermon' stuff.

FATHER GAILLAC: People mostly want to be good, they are trying to be good.

THERESE: That's only the ones going to mass all the time. Like my Nana. Mum used to say: Nana's always at confession, but why? What can she have to confess?

A pause, which is not at all awkward.

THERESE: I'm not trying to be good.

FATHER GAILLAC: Are you trying to be bad?

THERESE: I am bad.

FATHER GAILLAC: Who says?

THERESE: When I find him, I'll do it with my knife. I think about cutting him, killing him. All the time. That's why I need my knife.

FATHER GAILLAC: No, not in church. No knives, no blood, in

church. Isn't that why you're here, all of you, because you're safe from all that in here?

THERESE: Yeah, right: not in church. I wouldn't use it in church. But I'll need it on the street.

She holds out her hand for the knife. He hands it to her.

THERESE: Good job Nana's dead.

FATHER GAILLAC: If she'd known everything you told me she would have understood.

THERESE is unconvinced.

FATHER GAILLAC: Christ died for our sins. If Christ can forgive the man who did this to you, then he can forgive you – he can forgive you everything – everything that happened since. You only have to ask him.

She glances doubtfully at the confessional, the formality of it.

FATHER GAILLAC: You can say confession here. Sitting here. **(He means 'here, in this chair' (or wherever they are sitting or standing). He means the actual confessional itself is not essential for a confession.)** You only have to bow your head. **(A pause.)** 'May the Lord be in your heart and on your lips that you may readily – '

THERESE: **(rising)** No, sorry, Father – no.

She goes.

FATHER GAILLAC: **(after a pause)** Bless me, Father, for I have sinned. I kept my distance from the women. I was afraid to understand the women. I pitied their weakness; but I would not recognise their strength, the warmth and passion of their strength. Grandmothers, mothers, teenage girls: I was afraid to love these women.

Scene 6

Very early next morning. Dim light. FATHER GAILLAC is alone in some part of the church. He becomes aware of someone in the shadows. He feels uneasy.

FATHER GAILLAC: Hello? Someone there? (. . .) Who's there? **(Alarmed, angry, at there being no reply.)** Show yourself. Who are you?

The PENITENT shows himself. He wears a brimmed or peaked cap.

FATHER GAILLAC: What are you doing here?

PENITENT: Morning, Father.

FATHER GAILLAC: What do you want?

PENITENT: Just visiting, Father.

FATHER GAILLAC: How did you get in?

PENITENT: Just visiting God's house.

FATHER GAILLAC: The church has been locked since last night. How did you get in?

PENITENT: God's house belongs to everyone. You said that yourself, Father, on the radio the other day.

FATHER GAILLAC: Let me escort you to the door.

PENITENT: I want to say my confession, Father.

FATHER GAILLAC: I hear confession tomorrow afternoon.

PENITENT: Hear me now, Father. Or do you only have time for the whores?

The PENITENT goes to the confessional, and sits.

PENITENT: Bless me, Father, for I have sinned.

Although suspicious of the man, the priest feels bound to hear his his confession. He goes to the confessional, sits.

PENITENT: It is many years since my last confession.

FATHER GAILLAC: May the Lord be in your heart and on your lips that you may readily confess your sins –

PENITENT: Sin?

FATHER GAILLAC: – in the name of the Father, the Son, and the Holy Ghost. AMEN.

PENITENT: Sin's between man and God, right?

He's restless, faces away from the confessional.

FATHER GAILLAC: Confession is between man and God. Christ died for our sins, he takes our sins upon him. And forgives us.

Some slight sounds (Offstage) in the sleeping church.

PENITENT: Confession's secret, right?

FATHER GAILLAC: What's said in the confessional is never disclosed.

PENITENT: Yeah, you couldn't split on the ripper himself, right?

FATHER GAILLAC: Not after his confession, no.

PENITENT: They've got him all wrong, though. It's not like they say. He's cleaning the streets, that's all. Cleaning the streets.

FATHER GAILLAC: Confess your own sins, my son.

PENITENT: A woman's place is in the home.

FATHER GAILLAC: Lay your own sins before Christ.

PENITENT: A woman's place is in the sink. A woman's place is in the sewer.

FATHER GAILLAC: We can talk about this later. I think we need to talk, but this isn't the place. Can you come to my house later on this evening – the house next door, with the yellow shutters? Any time this evening – or any other evening? But for now, my son, confess your sins, for the Lord longs to meet you in sacrament –

PENITENT: He's doing the Lord's work, the ripper. Genevieve David!

THERESE comes on. Stays in the shadows.

PENITENT: I could have done that one. Could have done any of them. Watched them all, all the time.

FATHER GAILLAC: What are you confessing, my son? What are your sins?

PENITENT: Fuck them, screw them. He was cleaning the streets, that's all. He never ripped them, not like they said, nowhere near as bad. Cleaning up, that's all it is. I could have done that Genevieve. Tart – through and through. The way she bounced her tits, flashed her legs. They're all like that. Women – all of them: tarts – all of them. Women are like that – want that – like that –

PENITENT punches one fist into the the other hand – or hits out at a chair, the confessional screen, violently.

FATHER GAILLAC: Come and talk with me tonight. We can talk in private. The presbytery's next door.

PENITENT: **(in over this, impatient, loud)** 'For these and all my other sins, I'm very sorry.'

FATHER GAILLAC: Kneel down, my son.

PENITENT kneels down. FATHER GAILLAC not aware THERESE is close by.

FATHER GAILLAC: 'God the Father of Mercies, through the death and resurrection of his Son, has reconciled the world to himself and sent the Holy Spirit among us for the forgiveness of sins; through the ministry of the church may God give you pardon and peace, and I absolve you from your sins, in the name of the Father, and of the Son, and of the holy Spirit, Amen. (. . .) May the passion of the Lord Jesus Christ, the merits of the Blessed Virgin Mary and of all the saints and your own good deeds and sufferings grant you pardon, absolution, and the remission of your sins. Amen.'

FATHER GAILLAC says as much as is needed of the above absolution. During it, the PENITENT becomes aware of THERESE nearby. He sees her knife, she's about to stab him. The PENITENT rises to disarm, and defend himself.

FATHER GAILLAC: **(breaking off the absolution)** No! – no!

THERESE loses her grip for a split second – the knife is dashed from her hand. The PENITENT gets away, disappears.

FATHER GAILLAC: Not here. Not here.

THERESE: **(in over this)** Ripper!

FATHER GAILLAC: No!

THERESE: **(louder)** Ripper! **(Louder still – a warning to everyone in the church.)** Ripper!

FATHER GAILLAC is torn – the intruder is getting away – but there's the sanctity of the confessional, the altar space, of individual life. He stops her from following.

In the depths of the church (offstage) there are faint sounds, as the women wake, disturbed by THERESE's shouts.

THERESE: I could have killed him. I would have. **(Then, suddenly contrite, bows her head,as in confession.)** I would have killed him, Father.

As FATHER GAILLAC lays a hand on her hand, in absolution, there is the sound (offstage) of slow, heavy thuds on the outer doors. And as soon as the thuds start, there are cries (offstage) of 'Doors!', 'Doors!', 'Everybody on the doors!'. FATHER GAILLAC looks for the knife, picks it up, goes to the doors.

VOICE: **(offstage a loudhailer, outside the church)** Everybody on the street! Everybody on the street.

JOJO: **(offstage)** Go away, I've got a headache! We've all got a headache!

Offstage. Above the dull noise of the thuds, there is now the noise of splintering wood. The police have found a weak spot. They are breaking down the doors.

Scene 7

The WOMEN, FATHER GAILLAC, and RAYMOND. Each woman delivers her 'sentence' flatly. Raymond's sense of shock on witnessing the violence becomes more evident as his report continues.

JOJO: Josephina Maria Polidoro Orlando. Registered prostitute. Sicilian immigrant. Sixty years old. Present abode: 27 Zola Street. Previous convictions: soliciting; non-payment of fines; failing to appear as a witness; drunk and disorderly; re-setting; harbouring criminals; soliciting, soliciting, soliciting. Guilty as charged here with being present at the occupation of St Joseph's, resisting arrest –

RAYMOND: The big stick.

JOJO: – assault of police officers; lewd and abusive language; drunk and disorderly behaviour. Fined: five thousand francs, one month to pay.

RAYMOND: The big stick. The rod of iron.

DANIELLE: Danielle Marteau. Registered prostitute. Thirty-four years old. Three children. The first child was removed at birth, and sent for adoption. Present abode: Seven (a), Shoemaker Row. Previous convictions: soliciting, soliciting, soliciting. Manageress of the Cafe Cockatoo, 1972. License revoked for allowing soliciting on the premises: that is: running a brothel: that is: allowing her former sisters a chance to turn a trick. Guilty as charged here –

RAYMOND: There were ten cops to every whore. Ten cops to every whore.

DANIELLE: – with being present at the occupation of St Joseph's, resisting arrest, assault of police officers, attempt to bribe police officers, that is: refusing to open wide the lips in the black maria, refusing to open wide the legs in the black maria –

RAYMOND: They beat them with clubs. They beat them all over: on the head, on the breasts.

DANIELLE: Fined: eight thousand. Prison sentence suspended on the plea of the priest, Father Emile Gaillac.

FATHER GAILLAC: I tried to take some of the blows. I wanted the blows. But they handcuffed my arms behind my back, they shoved me down behind the chairs, they hadn't time for me. They had female fish to fry. There was nothing I could do.

LEILA: Lorraine Cartier. Street name: Leila. Registered prostitute. Arrived on the mainland from her native Corsica in 1968. 35 years old. Apartment 81, Block 12, Revolution Street. Previous convictions: possession of drugs, soliciting, harbouring a criminal, soliciting, drugs, soliciting, soliciting, soliciting. . . Fined eight thousand francs, one month to pay.

RAYMOND: They dragged them out by the hair. They rammed their clubs between their legs.

FATHER GAILLAC: A cordon round the church? A sea of scum around the church.

THERESE: Angelique Latour. Street name: Therese. Seventeen years old. Registered prostitute. Twelve Zola Street Lane. Previously of the House of Juvenile correction, Marseille.

RAYMOND: They were ready for her, they made a beeline for her. Two of them dragged her away by her legs, her head fell on the stone, they dragged her past the altar, they were pulling her legs wide. 'We'll split you between us', they said, 'how d'you like that, eh? Split you in two!'

THERESE: Guilty as charged: resisting arrest, causing assault and grievous bodily harm, possession of a stolen cheque book, possession of a knife. Three thousand francs, one month to pay. Prison sentence suspended after a plea by the priest, Father Emile Gaillac.

BRIGITTE: **(coming in over THERESE's last words)** Prenom: Brigitte. Surname not given. No fixed abode. According to medical report, 14 or 15 years old, four and a half months pregnant. To be placed immediately with the Sisters of the Immaculate Conception until the family can be traced.

RAYMOND: They threw them in the van. Their heads and bodies thrown against the sides of the van, against the iron bars of the windows of the van.

FATHER GAILLAC: Afterwards the Inspector unlocked my hands. He said they'd come into the church on hearing a disturbance. They'd heard cries for help. It was their duty to investigate.

RAYMOND: There was blood on the stones. There was blood on the carpet in front of the altar.

The 'Reportage' is over. The girls go off. FATHER GAILLAC and RAYMOND are back in the church, back to everyday work.

RAYMOND: Do you think that crazy was a cop?

FATHER GAILLAC signals that he doesn't think so, doesn't know.

Planted by the cops?

Again FATHER GAILLAC shrugs that he doesn't know.

You think he was the Ripper then?

FATHER GAILLAC: No. **(But he still seems unsure.)**

RAYMOND: There's not been another murder, Father, not since the strike. The girls are all back. Even that Brigitte – she's run away from the nuns. She's back on Zola street.

FATHER GAILLAC: The killer's still at large.

RAYMOND: It could have been him in the church that night. It must have been, Father.

FATHER GAILLAC: He was a penitent.

RAYMOND: He never came to confess! It was a trick! He'd no right to be there, and you caught him out. So he swore you to secrecy! He conned you to secrecy!

FATHER GAILLAC: That's not for me to judge.

They go.

Scene 8

BRIGITTE is back on Zola street.

BRIGITTE: Some of them are really nice when they see you're pregnant. One guy – I think he was a student: new jeans, new books, new beard – he freaked when he saw my belly. There were tears in his eyes. 'What's a girl like you – ?' A girl like me? A girl like me! **(She's neither hard, nor accusing.)** What about guys like you, then? What about guys like you?

The End